MISFIT

ECW PRESS

For Lynn:
A pleasure to offer this text
for you as a great fan of
your work.
All best,
Stephen Cain
01/04/22
Bar Italia.

TORONTOLOGY

STEPHEN CAIN

NATIONAL LIBRARY OF CANADA CATALOGUING IN PUBLICATION DATA

Cain, Stephen
Torontology

"A misfit book."
ISBN 1-55022-455-7

I. Title.

PS8555.A462T67 2001   C811'.54   C00-933255-3
PR9199.3.C34T67 2001

Edited by Michael Holmes / a misFit book
Cover and text design by Tania Craan
Cover photo by Rick / Simon
Author photo by Steve Venright
Layout by Mary Bowness

Printed by AGMV

Distributed in Canada by
General Distribution Services,
325 Humber College Blvd.,
Toronto, ON, M9W 7C3

Published by ECW PRESS
2120 Queen Street East, Suite 200
Toronto, ON M4E IE2
ecwpress.com

This book is set in Futura and Garamond.

PRINTED AND BOUND IN CANADA

The publication of *Torontology* has been generously supported by the
Canada Council, the Ontario Arts Council and the Government of Canada through
the Book Publishing Industry Development Program.

Canadä

FOR SUZANNE

CONTENT

5 X 4

Reef-bound rapture peril in the shell fishing for virtue in syntax lexiconical clusters of suckers & octaves the senate chamber lain with piece in your thyme or season of the bitch about the closing of the mind less frequent verbatim scansion conference of dunces with cup full of pop eye sam son source of power rangers looking for rings on eyebrow pencil chocolate.

[I.V. Lounge]

In Kathmandu did Chaka Khan a greatly measured moan by me. And what famed piece its power from a blast crouches [two words] bedly hands to be shorn. Settles on a het slack frau. No IUDs but in flings. Our compassion hit the light. A fan's speech should expend one's clasp or what's a semaphore. 'Til humane choices shake us, and we frown.

[Steve's house]

Too forsaken mermen disembodied heads & selkie sunburn clasping correction missed chief & smoking offshore prediction stranded by the main waiting for the go-ahead when silence is no longer a mystery & anything inside proves unsatisfactory can't swim as far as Krakatoa forbidding the rising of Mu sick patterns of engagement crystal rhythm laughter & forgetting euchre by the quartet suffrage & six is a fine number of problems how can you be sure bugging out & far from the ravening crowd.

[Wendy's cottage]

Sandinista revelation fraction serotonin cantina bifurcation fabulation fabrication media mediation meditation medication influenza intention intimidation imitation retina recommendation reconciliation inebriation pudenda participation precipitation preposition aporia anticipation animation altercation chora culmination configuration condensation.

[Brass Taps]

A hue as verdant as the hills are green a case of toms she only likes you for your eyes blood typed & wiped from the chin hand clasp shoulder rest & nothing's wrong but the will to sour the relation knocks the vote toward the missing variable by your side only offered patience rewarded by divine order a close conversation a fragrant catalyst.

[My place]

Error to err to air to heir to hair to there to here to fear to say it clear to lucky man to sealing fan to peerless plan to FM band to collective clan to poetic pan to a flawless tan to virgin steel to ardent zeal to loathsome meal to frequent deal to selfsame eel to a capacity to feel to sombre rite to healing light to a tempestuous night.

[Suzanne's place]

Tiger-stripe goosebump small frame cocaine red docs &
dyed-eyes missing the note qualify the presidential confess
deny deny & give the baby the answer it deserves smoking on
invisible structures 20 feet above the meltdown poisoning the
minds of children kissed on the bust want the write thing the
lucid syntax gravel-voiced & cough the mist the spray of
hoarse treading twice.

[The Horseshoe]

Wondering & wishing & washing & wasting & wandering
& wanking & whispering & wallowing & wanting &
walking & wowing & waking & wolfing & wavering &
waving & waxing & warning & whistling & weaving &
waiting & winding & withholding & writing & wringing &
warbling & warming & whiting & weighing & wagging &
waging & warding & warring & watching & watering &
wedging & welling & wedding & just being clear.

[Suzanne on the telephone]

Murphy's maw or speaking the unnameable when Malone
signals May Day fertility a scoundrel wagging the slag
convincing a fragile assemblage that decimation is in its best
interest hang-over solution left behind eating at the opening
of potentialities a Midtown collision Tom Dooley yearning
nothing matters & what if it did yes intrusion yes distraught
as I lay trying.

[Imperial Pub]

First it was there that time when over here hold it near or was it inside or look it's next to that under this moved to everywhere then on top of him nowhere else she was there we saw it here outside then right here then there see this it's here now it's nowhere everyone notices it's so there it will be here find it everywhere it's not gone it's inside here there always.

[College Streetcar]

1941: CITIZEN KANE
(ORSON WELLS): 199 MIN.

Citizen Cain to frenzy to record magnificence
Magnificence rumination impounded clairvoyance
Clairvoyance mastery serendipitous verbiage
Verbiage acclamation allows intricate conveyance
Conveyance control or record of complicity
Complicity removal transcendence monetary reward
Reward ribbons and bows to the audience
Audience approval fabrication coinage twice
Twice virtue thrice maximum discharge
Discharge weapon feigned outburst
Outburst celluloid heroism mediated clearly
Clearly compounds lack ichor and fluid
    Fluid transaction wells representation and flaws
    Flaws in crystal support thesis defence factor

Factor five facts or misappropriate gestures
Gestures to unreal city or calamitous orchids
Orchids found among rubble and floppy discs
Discs drive prices mulch mannerism
Mannerism platform of rehearsal fortunate
Fortunate vision exact toil and trial
Trial of veracity courage my beloved
Beloved catastrophe fondles fingers and blows
Blows leeward and steers to the right
Right leaning demagogues control movement
Movement overrated to sidewalk cyclists
Cyclists found in the month of May merry
    Merry trickster prances with coyote
    Coyote confusion of past parcels

Parcels bundled about the fountain of few
Few magicians and lesser amounts of tricks
Tricks turned near the doorstop to paradise
Paradise refrained and paradise cost
Cost to planets near the obit of foreign poets
Poets cancel subscriptions to the recitations
Recitations or breath-tracks on the crosswalks
Crosswalks supply treachery and tedious birthmarks
Birthmarks and justification of boudoir conversation
Conversation overflow for future reference
Reference jettisoned in favour of liquid
Liquid missile mars commode tragedy
    Tragedy of courtesans moustache monocle
    Monocle register or recognition of judgement

Judgement at Exodus catch the referent tonight
Tonight advertises possibility of reconciliation
Reconciliation to cryptic handwritten requests
Requests to nature windswept streets
Streets given ample opportunity to replicate
Replicate of Picasso fools only the wary
Wary and purge bilious shells of contentment
Contentment fallacy with media blitzkrieg voice-over
Voice-over required for acceptance and withdrawal
Withdrawal affects the sleeping patterns and cues
Cues the calls watches the crematorium
Crematorium soliloquies and frequent sonnets
    Sonnets written more than once less than zero
    Zero sum factor matters somewhat to myself

Myself the song sang of without recoil
Recoil to measurement last best answer
Answer the clone double the wager
Wager of sin games come before punishment
Punishment stops the odds against toys
Toys retrain the imagination
Imagination reversal galvanization of Zeus
Zeus villi electric biofeedback leaves of grass
Grass salt and wind-chime found without
Without it is within
Within the arrangement here there everywhere
Everywhere the question who should read
    Read in coffee shops recycled in pubs
    Pubs provide offspring of posey

Posey the query of chrysanthemums fragile
Fragile monosyllable wasted tongue
Tongue the opening remarks whettly so
So it is given to those who speak
Speak outside the discourse and retract
Retract the bass beat and give in to remote control
Control heretics and allow fortune to manifest
Manifest destination or argue the latter closure
Closure avoidance of consequential narrative
Narrative confinement disallow character
Character of inscrutable beauty foreshadow fallacy
Fallacy flow discovery of saints and canons
    Canons and sequences forbidden by the search
    Search the lexicon or indicate the glossary

Glossary framework ninety-nine tears
Tears the fabrication and maims the intention
Intention phallacy misrecognizes the graphics
Graphics are pleasant sometimes sole justification
Justification pricey at best roll the mice
Mice and mankind prudence last refuge
Refuge mortal remains constitutional crucible
Crucible critical slash at saviour
Saviour the flavour that expulsion brings
Brings ballast extra flesh on the side
Side short and tops infidel transit
Transit strike and elide the question
    Question majority evolution is a right
    Right to bereft right to canvas right to write

Write stuff get funds shadow the mysterious
Mysterious solution to card-carrying problems
Problems enter at uncalled for gatherings
Gatherings less a jurisdiction than imposition
Imposition of affliction and some left over
Over the reign waiting for the son
Son Sambo and bittersweet reflection
Reflection crystallize speculation and ovarian pontification
Pontification Simon Agonistes and morphic starts
Starts to bleed watch for the traces
Traces the outline and examines the paternal
Paternal gifts and requiem moonlight
    Moonlight the weight of words the beauty of reference
    Reference room silence wait for annunciation

Annunciation pray that head is forthcoming
Forthcoming whisper of pentecost and usury
Usury by the pound a rose that felt was hated
Hated exposition required despite the inclination
Inclination to observe the status of eyes
Eyes the equation deconstructs the formulation
Formulation of principles and secrete handshakes
Handshakes welcome instead of gifts or pegs
Pegs the process on the dancing angels
Angels and abstraction cause that inconvenience
Inconvenience store of maxims milks the probable
Probable backlash monster maelstrom or simple rhythm tic
    Tic tackles the rankles and manages victory
    Victory of race or say that Marinetti meant well

Well the issue is this perpetual boil
Boil bravo and Mexican screeds to solve boredom crossings
Crossings of significance multitudes migrate
Migrate the popular strong and not quite free
Free radicals and young radishes always possibilities
Possibilities of breakthrough always something new
New sensations of grand or even a few bucks
Bucks the system and watches for the result
Result the only answer the only creation of tao
Tao do right things that matter less than quantity
Quantity control or hearts that beat as one
One can stop the line at any time
    Time flies have affection for arrows
    Arrows the pass sometimes the answer is true

True light or false sight gemlike hardness
Hardness of virtue or purity of recombination
Recombination of elements and standard credit
Credit those who feel that their time has passed
Passed the examination but failed the grading
Grading is a given a grand adaptation of power
Power full of Irish mist and scarce midget misfits
Misfits of capricorn enemies of the date
Date those that lack all else but the ability of negation
Negation of consummation false gradation of such
Such sweet curios and asteroid quizzical formation
Formation compass of desire actress expression
 Expression lies against the predilection to confess
 Confess the probability await the penance randomly

Randomly the stars are now in transit
Transit of penis envies the renowned rival
Rival the best at the cusp of setback
Setback the remote and allow the rays to cathect
Cathect the object in retrieval or high heels salvation
Salvation in the form of a glowing cancer stick
Stick to the addiction and type slowly
Slowly or even thicker the quagmire of indecision
Indecision option paralysis frozen in the dice
Dice toss and serve with vinegar and oil
Oil the executioner and hope for slippage
Slippage crowned with fabrications and laurels
 Laurels and crags wonder whether positions are appropriate
 Appropriate curiosity and dangerous supplements

Supplements an absence and alleviates a yearning
Yearning for compassion deferment of gratitude
Gratitude for Stein and pathways that circle
Circle the repeated phrases and revoke the lexicon
Lexicon expectations drink a toast to the lost
Lost variable but best known for humility and creation
Creation in daze and lesser known cycles
Cycles back to you and moves the tide cautiously
Cautiously it meanders and then falls
Falls and other aquatic phenomena happily observed
Observed in natural habits and other vices
Vices are many and resistance is few
 Few participles and perilous voyages anticipated
 Anticipated streams of valour don't forget you

You are the reason that it exists
Exists at the beginning and the real solution
Solution of reflexivity is to ignore the nods
Nods to the author functioning RSVP immediately
Immediately too quick to tabulate the absolution
Absolution given and foolish decisions prevented
Prevented at the initial exposure of folly
Folly be praised and raised to optimum sight
Sight return and feed the very respected fountain head
Head right in and don't wait for the rest
Rest awhile and claim priority in the pool
Pool the resources and dance to the tune
 Tune to the key of A and then blow against the main
 Main reason cannot be explicated expect no less

Less is not more ignore the total Aryan state
State belief and press on and then to begin press on
On that day you shall become as able as Kane....

1971: A CLOCKWORK ORANGE (STANLEY KUBRICK): 137 MIN.

A clockwork arrangement blowing the problem
Problem being matters left to fortitude
Fortitude arctic expression not seagull arabesque
Arabesque movement folding tents in the night
Night music that Max Ernst would avoid painting
Painting the corner before the floor is laid
Laid daily ennui appears nonetheless
Nonetheless matters are better than expectations
Expectations revealed so discard any innuendo
Innuendo catalyst an island that Odysseus avoids
Avoids the calamity the cat came back
Back to basic-training doesn't mean preparation
    Preparation for the abyss toil in the mail
    Mail strike a person person fabrication true

True to the ultimate rage for order
Order order the recipe for blue guitar Sundays
Sundays on the weekend before the last evening
Evening tide pool verbalization stands to reason
Reason the season for disbelief
Disbelief the participation of mannered maxims
Maxims of amber versions that collapse with Troy
Troy the turrets that I walk nightly
Nightly to master weekly to request
Request the revision and historicize the equation
Equation quantum formulate the bastardization quite
Quite the quandary to spell the bee blue
    Blue sixteen the call waiting effect
    Effect the change and mind your dollars

Dollars make sense when anal cues move
Move the nice to consider palmistry and coins
Coins the phase and Kuhn continuums falter
Falter to shuffle the desks and ink wells shatter
Shatter the prism to scatter the colour
Colour outside the lines and expire
Expire to progress to qualify a chemistry
Chemistry biology a lyric taste of empiricism
Empiricism of tyranny an incarceral subject
Subject to power fascinated by Foucault and them
Them a quarry or perhaps only a foe pause
Pause then continue the debate without cause
　　Cause no questions answer no probability
　　Probability of reception minimal write anyway

Anyway the poem continues without the reader
Reader response and fragment policy revoked
Revoked ticket to ride and day trip the walrus
Walrus vermin or merely the mites of right
Right shifting can be the diamond mine singer
Singer and dancer who can tell the difference
Difference Easter 1916 and beauty born of chaos
Chaos of expression masques of impersonal rendering
Rendering the swans song mute fairy fabrication
Fabrication of beasts that slouch toward dawn
Dawn patrol parameters question boundaries
Boundaries of light and calm the crashing wave
　　Wave length of expectation cull the ego bright
　　Bright resounding event then realize terrible terrible

Terrible grafting heads explode despite solace
Solace of black debt acknowledge inspiration
Inspiration of language Ulysses ere returning
Returning the favoured genre and modes matter
Matter of too much acid and too little base
Base the structure on myth then watch for implosion
Implosion certainly but notwithstanding Achilles
Achilles dismemberment and query Osiris to follow
Follow the flow and stitch the pieces flawless
Flawless Odin of frankincense and mere gold
Gold age ravenous for glory buttered for Elysium
Elysium magnetism summer fields of bliss
    Bliss not chosen but edible qualities persist
    Persist and decline the fall of imperial homes

Homes are not habitations nor burrows salvation
Salvation sanity freedom to move
Move the object immobile and resist
Resist the gender and trouble the closet
Closet desire or disguise the impulsion
Impulsion of transgression dress the part
Part the folds Butler leaves to barbed wire
Wire the message and wait for response
Response to trouble ignored consummation
Consummation achieved despite the odds
Odds fabricate freak show night town travelled
Travelled in youth and sequestered in obsolescence
    Obsolescence entailed in production practical
    Practical logic for simplistic organisms

Organisms fail the comprehensive exam
Exam anxiety Art Bergman convalescence
Convalescence sustain fraternal patricide
Patricide oh brother the two that are acquitted
Acquitted wolves under the skin covered by genes
Genes split and are developed by scientific beauty
Beauty the truth of negative capacity
Capacity for revulsion to Lovecraft scenario
Scenario qualified by foreboding often sincere
Sincere fear but busted by boredom
Boredom a simple lullaby craving contagion
Contagion pillowcase sorry for treatment
    Treatment when reserved but otherwise wait
    Wait forward to coming experience

Experience the perspective denied
Denied setbacks prosper even within spheres
Spheres music dancing crystal apparatus lost
Lost the bear rings witches gather this evening
Evening tide oven watching Calypso sweat
Sweat masks the circles that manifest
Manifest destinies that signal revolution
Revolution in subconsciousness dedicated to many
Many nights returning visited with fingers
Fingers snap happiness momentary and often
Often praise the memory but seldom the image
Image this photographs of salt mines unreal
    Unreal metropolis Baudelaire foresight
    Foresight ignored but read about in school

School daze fondest remora emerges quickly
Quickly erased discovery flora and fondness
Fondness for Nicky could be real
Real presently the suburb gains momentum
Momentum bicycle the namesake greeting
Greeting the criticism boldly removing
Removing reference applauded by strangers
Strangers written for plus of course myself
Myself electric Brooklyn Bridge hymn
Hymn bodies and hands clasped presently
Presently the vision drains the experience
Experience the jettison the flotsam circus
    Circus welcome the reminder the lazy eye
    Eye the television failed spell roll again

Again the stanza recoils offering bliss
Bliss disavows cancer maps head wounds
Wounds regained by prayer released slovenly
Slovenly abode seldom resembles treatment
Treatment racist but friendly sometimes
Sometimes eggplant quiver justified by coasting
Coasting the surf pebbles shaped like fish
Fish for responses straight vinegar possession
Possession deferred constantly temptation futile
Futile smoking through screens kitchen doorway
Doorway movement a morning smell of orange....

RUSSIAN DOLLS

GERTRUDE STEIN
"I am I because my little dog knows me."

I am I because my dog knows me

I am I because my dog knows

I am I because dog knows

I am I because dog

I am I because

I am I

I am

I

quote

quote context

you quote context

do you quote context

how do you quote context

how do you quote except out of context

"How else do you quote except out of context"
GEORGE BOWERING

1977: STAR WARS (GEORGE LUCAS): 121 MIN.

Star doggie style or Russian formal
Formal position taken but then necks collide
Collide from the beginning and then start
Start sixty nining and answer tender buttons
Buttons bothered by downy ferns and tips
Tips the ballast but denies paternity
Paternity can be sweet but spray the pearl
Pearl collars and visual rifles breathe
Breathe shallow and think only of self
Self fashioning puns proliferate simply
Simply the repetition of performativity recalled
Recalled before sleep continued in morning
    Morning stiffness stretch the yawn discretely
    Discretely the tapping renunciation shadow

Shadow the nose not too loud
Loud gesture howl the academic gridlock
Gridlock Coney Island minefield anyway
Anyway praise not spritely jazz the community
Community values those who participate in karma
Karma shape shifting comes and goes
Goes like thus window the mystery prank
Prank parks mentioned once then at bat
Bat bell tower small fries and Stalin slips
Slips to the surface whisper beverage and ice
Ice the enemy fast food utopias and cars
Cars resemble social formation not pleasant
    Pleasant over-population less than perpetual
    Perpetual miscommunication listen in stereo

Stereo hubcaps nickel and dime to expiration
Expiration of modernity the man is right
Right away and presently everything fails
Fails the middle period of ignorance outside
Outside smile think for days trickle the flood
Flood gateway to revelation weary response rider
Rider sees seas and stations to stations seized
Seized by the birthright cancelled before midnight
Midnight continues easily arranged before sentence
Sentence structured but lost in the recollection
Recollection of time dismissed poor probability
Probability of stars funds are funny
    Funny glimmer zones are frequently repealed
    Repealed to production venomous miscues sound

Sound of filling follows chalked until June
June memories consider the evidence
Evidence of standardization god's wounds
Wounds the incision zip-locked to dance
Dance the queen and flip the sparrow
Sparrow denouement quay to puzzle
Puzzle the problematic sounds almost mute
Mute recovery foreshadows the tyranny
Tyranny of multiplicity ask for beverage
Beverage of choice often acclimatized for spring
Spring forward fall back to static
Static flexation weary diode of May
    May be forthcoming but perhaps not now
    Now is the winter of discothèque

Discothèque a serial novel by you too
Too bad gal and a half fractions fracture
Fracture the rapture and comment on results
Results of cry-baby queries extra fine
Fine the manor but lease the compulsion
Compulsion to marry but seldom smarter
Smarter than spoken word but equally null
Null set the time to recall and revolution
Revolution of language and then Steve barters
Barters the communication and riddle me this
This word belongs here but not always there
There she goes there she goes again
    Again Apollo but sometimes the goddess of chance
    Chance meeting but then what's not true

True paternity belongs in enclosures
Enclosures of fortitude smiles on a whim
Whim the fancy and absorbent tissue spleen
Spleen is a humour so is Stove Top stuffing
Stuffing the envelope pressed against the device
Device of revelation Bakhtin has a conversation
Conversation of dialogues everybody's happy
Happy hilarious or on occasion drunk
Drunk on the ritual sorry the shades don't show
Show the blood and chase away mother
Mother of invention witty yet dies
Dies daily and ships never regain direction
    Direction to islands nymphs lips are pressed
    Pressed so sweetly the invocation is forsaken

Forsaken mermaid the chapel withdraws
Withdraws the climax he never loved the king
King frenzy long life long rest
Rest of the confession can be considered small
Small comfort and your burial before birth
Birth of tragedy the felines crush skulls
Skulls begin the sentence but lacks execution
Execution of primates Shakespeare is forthcoming
Forthcoming monologue stammered among courtiers
Courtiers with chest-ache acknowledge no leash
Leash of winged soles incense brazier found
Found the cloven-hoof dined with the devil
    Devil the egg a hard-boiled detective novel
    Novel of sentiment don't forget the thesis

Thesis statement approved for recession
Recession Betty Boop eyebrow resolution
Resolution played out for the coronation
Coronation mounted by canine foot patrol
Patrol the whereabouts but avoid the scene
Scene of symphonies a fantastic iceberg
Iceberg let us dance and let us frolic
Frolic certainly fast the box is empty
Empty discourse asterix the explorer
Explorer navigator search the engine
Engine of perpetual motion nonexistent
Nonexistent personage characters can converge
    Converge author reader function historical fact
    Fact of the matter Isis and Horus reunited

Reunited with my baby blue protracted narrative
Narrative cybernetics and artificial intelligence
Intelligence a question of what you know
Know the culmination is coming fast
Fast and hard spew the blanched cells
Cells of socialism keep the faith
Faith in super monsters that bear the blows
Blows before the breeze of democracy
Democracy the only justification of wars....

1979: APOCALYPSE NOW
(FRANCIS FORD COPPOLA): 153 MIN.

Apocalypse presently best foot forward
Forward to designation encrypt the rest
Rest the turbine and excite the auto
Auto eroticism hearts follow the mind
Mind your head two steps to the left
Left behind on the hot plate of life
Life given to the holy inappropriate
Inappropriate jester hangs for folly
Folly the footstep that falls lightly
Lightly embraced and planted in the face
Face the fiction all writing dries
Dries the dishes that centipedes provoke
    Provoke jansenism papish plots remain
    Remain in the blight all the girls reward

Reward mantra recite twice and pick up sticks
Sticks in the throat thanks to spanish fly
Fly from persecution manna will appear
Appear to signify but only in retrospect
Retrospect film festival etiquette
Etiquette can be discovered in likely places
Places the cart before the chorus
Chorus lines taken with mirror and razor blade
Blade sprinter this comes later
Later it was revealed that the horses bolted
Bolted to the floor the television miscarried
Miscarried proposals tabled until infinity
    Infinity is needless to say a long time
    Time to reap time to plow through volumes

Volumes spoken but what have I said
Said before and presently again the interrogation
Interrogation of subject positions prosper
Prosper without books staves or bells
Bells the feline requiem for mice
Mice are nice that's what they say
Say without reference but mean with presence
Presence intense purpose of aquatic flora
Flora and revenge bastions of virtue
Virtue of Farley mohawk twelve years old
Old exegesis is overlaid by illumination
Illumination in library firefly moth trap
    Trap the particles but ignite the source
    Source of muse factory a deathly secret

Secret the ace of spades and win the game
Game if you are does are dear
Dear John this is not a reference to you
You stay for the completion therefore are brave
Brave words and bloody knuckles explode
Explode the sign but stop when Levi-Strauss appears
Appears to transcend sometimes optical illusions rule
Rule the neighbourhood of forgotten scribes
Scribes respond to light or heavy stimulus
Stimulus converted to sound poetics or performance
Performance of several horsemen just fucking around
Around the mulberry bush the hollow men dance
    Dance the regal canto that pounds the bass
    Bass thing knocked twice about the head

Head given until dead now what's the score
Score the winning goal against formalist Russians
Russians await the motif cyclical
Cyclical headstrong opponent a fairy tale ending
Ending the enterprise bob to the beat
Beat on the brat with a baseball bat
Bat ten never reach the line up
Up to circumstance but the circus is in town
Town and gown betrayal a Pinter for your trouble
Trouble in the hen house foreshadows foxes
Foxes ravines and the occasional eggs
Eggs the process to its potential epiphany
    Epiphany translucent and somewhat lucid
    Lucid dreaming of her all the night

Night lines the estuary lotus position
Position the petals to heat the bathtub
Bathtub gin the beverage of choice
Choice of the lost generation an absinthe presently
Presently a black olive migraine
Migraine the fields of undergraduates nicely
Nicely the offers present themselves
Themselves the nemesis of degradation
Degradation is ultimately forestalled
Forestalled conclusion wait until the term is over
Over and ran with forgive the bibliography
Bibliography projected into space
    Space the white room repainted white
    White knights and satin cenotaph newspapers

Newspapers the floor but drops reveal colour
Colour inside the outlines but blur the border
Border skirmish results appear in code
Code principle give nothing away
Away yet far the beast is slouching north
North rebellion the city at the end of things
Things that make one go Hume
Hume the philosopher respected without reading
Reading this morning sputter over coffee
Coffee the acknowledged gift of imperialism
Imperialism I meant T.E. Lawrence desperation
Desperation accursed drought of monsoons
    Monsoons predate patrician nonsense
    Nonsense she washed the scent from her eyes

Eyes the clock and punches the machine
Machine impression madness soon occurs
Occurs despite the medication take two more
More than lithium when does it stop
Stop the insanity provisos appropriated by idiots
Idiots despised but they buy poetry too
Too quick for retraction the Crimean war begins now
Now discontented seasons of prosperity
Prosperity neglected for academic futures
Futures the location that paths lead to often
Often forgotten persuasive fundamentalists resound
Resound the effort of breaking crystal
    Crystal awareness of nymphs and mints
    Mints the coinage but forgets the bill

Bill the patient participant rapidly
Rapidly excused for vampire worldliness
Worldliness of virtue a plain dealer succeeds
Succeeds despite the sods a grassy grimace
Grimace the thief of frozen vegetables
Vegetables in the white room can of corn reminder
Reminder to make everything phosphate free
Free to the lover the poet or madman
Madman enterprise continued next serial
Serial Chinese boxes look for inner prizes
Prizes order over all states of being
Being green of jeans an argument for ontology
    Ontology asking epistemology for purpose
    Purpose to frolic with French dolphins and whales

Whales in the memory of a childhood holiday
Holiday looking for a place in the sun
Sun of guns a solar predicament unexpected
Unexpected remedy for seasickness discovered
Discovered continents Atlantis of the psyche
Psyche without Hyperion writing the epic right
Right direction but wondering about predilection
Predilection for nylons and tights discouraged
Discouraged formalist expressive gymnastic display
Display the legs desired but subtract the middle
Middle English queries about some thane I ate
Ate at the opening but stayed for the envelope
    Envelope sealed similarly but rings worn through
    Through the evening and towards the eighties

Eighties revival or a chronicle of fraternity
Fraternity of equality without much liberty
Liberty silvers the pay-check but sings low
Low lower lowest of the low lowing on loan
Loan a credible expression to the haiku fabricator
Fabricator of fabulous aphorisms see above
Above reproach below the litmus test
Test the waters for johns but flamingos go
Go flaming into that good night
Night recollection of woods and mongrels
Mongrels and mastiffs know a cur for all
All considered that's how the mind works
Works responsibly but stops the event now....

deClerambault's Syndrome

"Give me a Leonard Cohen afterworld
So I can sigh eternally
I'm so tired I can't sleep
I'm a liar and a thief"

— K.C. "Pennyroyal Tea" —

PEACH

Assume the beauty position
Once broken all is fair game
Seals are oily mammals
Leather or lubrication
And that's what signifies
Italianicity

A triadic salute
So sore the memory burns
Bovine foot fetish
A perfect placenta
Separate peaceable gnostics
Promenade promises
Lifting wings a bowie knife hero
Joe College sister boom pa-pa
Perfection is an unpleasant state

Black and white and
Naturally
Red all over
Amphibious breathing
Sometimes they come
Back

      Flaccid militaristic response
      If Fergie eats that will you
      Rubberized beneath the surface
      Okay okay an unhealthy fraternity
      Clambering monkeys
      Lipping leggings
      Short at the sides & long down my
      Back
      Scarsdale clinical excision

PRETTY MONEYEYES

Faciality a fond recollection
Blue-eyed parole
On the knees soften
Guzzle the tragedy
Islamic fundamentals
A cherry lifesaver dissolving

> Keeping the cryptogram
> Concussion green age
> It's alright if Prospero goes
> Dire straightening
> Some flings cannot be solved
> Pentagram rebus rubik cubed
> Calamity Jones
> Nothing is more important
> Than writing

MOURNINGSIDE

Altar the circumstance
Mornings beside
Say it if you mean it
Gentlemen prefer bonds
Gunning for removal
A novelty we race to replace

> In a town of kings
> The popper is special
> Speaking in tongues
> The Clash & a horny horse
> Missing the connection
> Mired in the mundane
> Kinky curls
> An infant discourse
> I can't give you a blowjob tonight

THREE MILES OF BAD ROAD

A furtive fister
Toys with the probability
Similar to that
But different than bliss
Too long in the steam
Did Juno know Circe

        Conversations fill
        That was one moment
        This is another
        Selective memory
        Never understood the cul de sac
        A Parkdale escapade
        Virilio vector
        Fixative for transgression
        deSade situation

ENGLISH SUEDE

A brotherhood of bores
Dogman Ishtar
Octopussy dressing gown
An empty fishtank
Regional rectum
These are the days I feel cold

> Nine completions
> Of childhood rivalry
> Bareback computations
> Hair in the mouth that bit me
> This number has been changed
> To protect the inner sense
> Similarly the action
> Rewards the effort
> Betrayal offers anecdotes

VANILLA

The lure of the white wyrm
Somewhat feline scratching
The purpose
Planned obvious essence
Incensed sponge impressions
Michael Robartes & the Dancer

                    Too particular about viscosity
                    Strange lingering of Irish Spring
                    Various nexus
                    Photographic nightingale vessels
                    Seminal experience mont blanc
                    A key in the hand
                    A chest release
                    Secret success
                    Finnish when you parted

THE INDUSTRIAL REVOLUTION

Eagled inner thigh
Indelible
Scar to warning
Gypsum-eyed naiad
Engineer of limbic souls
Light between finger escapes

Glacial abode sunbite
Nights on Bold Mountain
Subway sinister masquing
No evil I-Ching
Phallic pool conquest
Let me count the plays
Carrying like explosives
Mine your or a
Laurentian pathos of power

GUIDED BY VOICES

Opening containers under pressure
Rainwater immersion
Bathe or salve or recoil
Moles are small creatures
Solar flare lunatic
Damien's is the only position

Expulsion of vitality
Can't respect what you don't
Betty or Varronian
Sad slack attitude
Small death with your boots on
Footprints on the sealing
Mixmaster journalism walkabout
Too harsh in the recollection
A Kleenex will clarify mistakes

CHLOE

The unbearable rightness of seeing
Slippery borders
A gambol irresistible
Deep blackness revealing quality
Quizzical communication
Listen to the beat of separate starts

> The difference extremes us
> Shakedown Tacoma trailer rainfall
> A penitent desire for servitude
> Surreal conductive subjectivity
> Cloying to what shepherd
> Whistle stop situation
> The process of time
> Drastic measures meant
> So long marry and

Manhattan island of the mind ignites perfumed
Perfumed mistress just clap for service
Service vectors and chaos patterns curve
Curve tangles of angels and shortened thrones
Thrones of dominion jewelled for the appearance
Appearance of godhead or the absent ego
Ego of orientalism some tastes do vary
Vary very necessary to juxtapose morality
Morality a quandary of dry goods maximized
Maximized for the biofeedback transcendence brings
Brings spectres of marks ghosts of graduation
Graduation celebration a wake for youthful aspirations
    Aspirations of mermaids rolling your trousers
    Trousers singing to oneself the daily bitterness

Bitterness of stockings bipeds do age
Age of eclectic lifestyles prefab sexual dissidence
Dissidence or transgression an A plus affirmative
Affirmative retraction or excuse the muse
Muse as expected but discard Rodin's physique
Physique examined and no flaws on the phallus
Phallus centred on society aim to please
Please the butter a Gary Glitter arrangement
Arrangement of positions a lotus of landings
Landings predicted but coming down is hard
Hard wears well and continues to be popular
Popular reception arboreal rainforest coastline
    Coastline patrol the limbs for parasites
    Parasites maintained 'pataphysically smash the subject

Subject to whimsy a speculation of optics
Optics a nervous gesture predicted frequently
Frequently the choice of experience meeting
Meeting the lemonade prospectus early
Early morning confrontations a mirror of defense
Defense of weight a cerebral hoodwinking
Hoodwinking an odd word to start sentience
Sentience a self-fulfilling prophecy
Prophecy surprised by sin a tangential oracle
Oracle of delving the accidental contraction
Contraction of distemper spleen the cavern
Cavern the Platonic reversal nominally present
    Present and accounted forthright among the several
    Several microscopic tragedies a cosmic miscue

Miscue the recollection all sounds to blame
Blame the sinister mystery of minstrelsy
Minstrelsy said ten times quickly
Quickly follows the intoxication blindly
Blindly readership limitation is taxed
Taxed to what design a turgid reminder to placate
Placate the reading process consider vocabulary
Vocabulary learned merely to obscure dialogue
Dialogue fabrication bookmarked for excision
Excision fusion operator stuck in Mobile
Mobile rodents the scattering of wisdom
Wisdom governed by strict structures
    Structures of feeling a ray of insight
    Insight of the frontlines avoid Rupert Brooke

Brooke shields the answers from the translation
Translation of Sanskrit crib notes to the Odyssey
Odyssey of vacuum two seas of tranquillity
Tranquillity of repose a Torontonian lunar eclipse
Eclipse restless inmates by a narrow fraction
Fraction stability decides who gets pi
Pi the repeating decimal after the fact
Fact through friction sexual tension remains
Remains of the play enter the forest covertly
Covertly a trenchcoat indicates voyeurs
Voyeurs certainly count yourself as one
One marble contemplating the works of giants
    Giants and multi-coloured articles of clothing
    Clothing the fortunate for the Queen Street parade

Parade past the barn mediating mortality
Mortality of autumn the fresh smell of ocean
Ocean encounter a campfire of driftwood
Driftwood music and pyres of waxen dragons
Dragons tambourines and golden chalice maidens
Maidens cut hair in the perilous chapel
Chapel hillside rendezvous ignore the pavement
Pavement expressionism abstracted to closure
Closure of memory the hyacynth girl in pearls
Pearls of glass eyes that record transgression
Transgression of hiking trails a quagmire of salt
Salt the worthiness obesity crowned in anger
    Anger a basement dweller and sidewalk cyclist
    Cyclist respect watching for floating barns

Barns and the collection of Curnoe's stamps
Stamps across the ceiling destroying concentration
Concentration camps nearby and sulks in his tent
Tent caryatid sculpted heads held high
High at times but mostly just smoking moonshine
Moonshine await exhuming of exquisite corpse
Corpse of pleas know the ire of sonatas
Sonatas heard through the fingers of repression
Repression of quiet mechanisms totemistic slogans
Slogans engineered to hunt souls
Souls and their solutions to graceful footsteps
Footsteps echo the dusty streets of Manhattan....

1982: BLADE RUNNER
(RIDLEY SCOTT): 118 MIN.

Blade consumer a sideshow expectation met
Met the parents but hated the dinner
Dinner recital a boiled egg sandwich and toast
Toast the bridegroom and smoke in the cloakroom
Cloakroom tableau caught with reddened digits
Digits accounted for but lost track of time
Time gentlemen and goodnight ladies goodnight
Goodnight and farewell to the paperback prince
Prince was a toy dog on wheels
Wheels with the implication for transportation
Transportation a proper title for mixed manuscripts
Manuscripts proof-read and house set in order
    Order the execution and anticipate front-row seats
    Seats four comfortably but some sit on laps

Laps taken for those who were not in uniform
Uniform conclusion a caucus that avoids mountains
Mountains of my mind rejected at the outset
Outset of Vancouver reappraisal of housing
Housing a hangover and a slight addiction to orgasm
Orgasm trinity and ten lovers to the mile
Mile stoned in fields where acres rare meat
Meat never passed the lips but much wine was involved
Involved in the conspiracy and can't drive standard
Standard size but an inch more would please
Please refrain from flipping the burger master
Master of action and a beautiful disposition
    Disposition can be observed as a virtue
    Virtue merely a masque for bored revellers

Revellers out past curfew a Jacobean declaration
Declaration of intention or self-reflexive exercise
Exercise your right to dote on fawn-eyed objects
Objects to the insinuation that genders are stable
Stable the studs and don't waste the seed
Seed discontent and provoke necessary controversy
Controversy an aborted bon mot a treacherous body
Body of residence an underground expensive enterprise
Enterprise a lauded vessel of caramelized speciality
Speciality of embrace kissed before the expiry
Expiry date the subject that never went well
Well well Guelph water the troughs for foresight
    Foresight is only to be expected somewhat prerequisite
    Prerequisite for generalized ambidextrous entertainers

Entertainers exasperate an unsettled situation
Situation recollection never the same thrice
Thrice conceived is twice sodomized blatantly
Blatantly a perfection of sleeping bodies
Bodies of an animal not wanting an offspring
Offspring forward a temporal version of temperance
Temperance is preferred but is never mandatory
Mandatory conscription of periodic phenomenon
Phenomenon phylum or genesis of linguistics
Linguistics courses urgently simple mathematics
Mathematics never excelled but was able to pass
Pass the collection on the left hand side
    Side with Satanists nothing's dangerous anymore
    Anymore the setting was a wasteland of opportunity

Opportunity knocks on the school of hardness
Hardness a theme song of mythology many-minded
Minded the establishment who's watching the followers
Followers question the motivation at this point
Point the way to vision ascribed to Paul of Vienna
Vienna ice cream toasted Susie is my sweetheart
Sweetheart and mindful of dissident beautification
Beautification of tabernacles a slide guitar required
Required for the ceremony manicured properly
Properly attired for the formal new criticism
Criticism taken lightly not a word is spoken
Spoken in the wheel of fortune symbolically it's fictional
Fictional struggle for the ego of playgrounds
Playgrounds abound with forgotten sea monsters

Monsters should be available to most authors
Authors a scenario motivates a keyboard functional
Functional comparative literature a dead fellowship
Fellowship of trolls lips serviced upon request
Request the intermission that royalty allows
Allows a wish for cyclical end-stopped lines
Lines the bathtub with sealant touches the faucet
Faucet effeminate a kinder bourgeois affectation
Affectation sampled for a tuneful requiem
Requiem transubstantiation investigation
Investigation tragedy a golden falcon released
Released without hail the sovereign's body unmarked
Unmarked assignments a Damocles situation
Situation stable with critical brevity forthcoming

Forthcoming prophecy bringing it to a close
Close but no die monster die
Die the barter that can never withhold
Withhold services but then who's hurting who
Who by the fireplace pretending to experience
Experience always preferred consumer astonishment
Astonishment reconciled with late humanism
Humanism a thousand monkeys typing away
Away and far and a similar drum beat
Beat box baby on a Saturday night
Night in the bathroom setting chain reactions
Reactions to the actions set in motion
    Motion an oceanic perspective I find lacking
    Lacking motivation the race is certainly on

On the side of good semiotic analysis
Analysis of internal organs awaiting removal
Removal poison ivy web site ministry
Ministry of Love and several other commotions
Commotions on the pathway of righteousness
Righteousness a probable cause of divorce
Divorce from reality and question all epistemology
Epistemology breakthrough invoking a cypher revolution
Revolution assured by rug-burn advocates
Advocates of contagion a coded frequency
Frequency of zip codes bootlegging the salvation
Salvation or redemption don't waste good words
    Words and angel food cake how many variations
    Variations and worrisome presence of rash

Rash decisions predict rapid distortions
Distortions of intimacy mirror ball encounters
Encounters of the first kind but then what's not
Not necessarily an issue but can provoke nonetheless
Nonetheless the rumour spreads that it sucks
Sucks at the heart of a long distance runner....

PRISON TATTOOS

A TEAR

one slides
one lingers

a fabric causation
an even split

in memory of loss
a solitary cellmate

never issued from i
witnessed several before

colourless in the dark
an accidental birthmark

sometimes involuntary
incarceration serendipity

pumice the traces
the miss of fingerprints

blueprint rendezvous
the corner of christy

pits the need to the crossfire
scattered evenly over oceans

me & baby jesus

A SNAKE

been down this
metaphor before

sometimes one
but eve has been known

to lie against a telephone
receiver of bad karma

shining on the forest
of spit & spite

wreckage at the cross
roads waver in the heat

spotting pads & toxic
shockwave filtration

plants the cede
in a sleeping mind

field of copies perhaps
one of the wonders of creation

or phallacy flotsam

A ROSE

never given
still remains one

is & is once more
making chaucer anew

pigment for painting
the selfsame welkin

ringing the wrong
answering machine

only a few hours a
part of the hole

addition of submission
caterwauls or nine

tales of brave ulysses
periwinkle hercules

missionary statement
of intentionality scaring

scars of illumination
too bold a process

which defines a tattoo anyway

A SKULL

bones witness
clutching absent coins

hilarious party-stopper
blue-eye-balled

the damp petition
towards abolishment of bondage

gearing up for dedication
to the wrong song

bird waking early again
fucking things up

yours is the sweetest
presence i've shared

life cycles only about
fifteen minutes away

with that anything is possible
consequence denial of connections

or the day the universe changed
makes me want to sing

louie lou reed

A CROSS

a great divide
between futurity

and the past particles
imparfait situation

desperate despite
pleasured principalities

of what's ours & what
we want to take

a noman crusade
or mule's quest

for fire or something else
which burns stubbornly

futile persistence
silent sentencing

operatic scenario
making shadows

where none should fall
on your knees

the seizure is all mine

A DAGGER

makes incisioned decisions
one-sided double-edged

serrated smile or
similar simile

like the other evening
but less relaxed

invigilation refusal
to take sideburns

a little greyer than before
it didn't really matter

with less artful
dodger of critical questions

the reason for meeting
halfway to paradise

by the headboard light
escaping between fingers

the liquid sub rosa
if you're a pynchon situation

then i'm the breton response

A NAKED WOMAN

not objective desire
nor the sole recollection

more wonderful than imagined
geography of presence

tense chambers
all six loaded

with liquor
withdrawal & a shaky

signpost below
mason & dixon

lineage traced with palms
flattened against ears

tongued before but
a purgatory renewal

of lost fabricated
fantasies fulfilled

just an expulsion of tissue
i'm still young

i still want to say something

A HEART

misplaced by listening
to the wrong side

shift the aural
to oral & it becomes

clear warm & wasted
on the grounded shifting

before the stretching
happy just to be there

there she says
sensitive to the position

i advocate freedom
to feel the power

full of passion
anyone can see

saw the potential
too early in the energy

vamping the mirrored
glass between my fingers

a head on my chest

BARBED WIRE

a nickname previous
incarnation as a venus

phoenix insurrection
holy devoted

place in your kalendar
booth bartending

the stray shapes
and testing all options

too often in cabs
lighting cigarettes against

despairing of returning
occurrence lucky seven

westward planning
too far in advances

ignored or else filed away
for future recall

it wasn't fare at all
bets are off

'cause i want you silly

SOME LETTERS

are penned not to be read
in a prison of self

made illusion seem real
can't trust my memory

words spoken in vain
regrettable journey to the

group of seven location
on the body of knowledge

that it hurts before it heals
a stable discourse

can be offered like
throats legs & heels

a welcome connection
over phone lines

safety in sexuality
walking past midnight

hard to let it be
i love the lure of language

along your lips

1992: THE ADJUSTER
(ATOM EGOYAN): 102 MIN.

The adjuster of technologies and astrological surveillance
Surveillance calamity and all my work goes well
Well the ground-swell for turpitude but carefully
Carefully the longest bits are accomplished first
First of the mastheads and last call rings true
True to the wife a mimetic experience lasting
Lasting the time for gestation but no longer
Longer than expected for the time to make a beverage
Beverage should not be underrated nor vitamin E for skin
Skin the protection but understand the lips
Lips and the repetitive seals that merely bark
Bark of dogwood represents a cure-all redistribution
    Redistribution of wealth some girls are bigger than others
    Others have the inspiration but waste it on intoxication

Intoxication roadblock and icy receptions consequentially
Consequentially an octogenarian appearance expected
Expected to heal but some scarring inevitable
Inevitable shoestring production of excess
Excess of affection some guys have all the luck
Luck of the withdrawal avoid paternity in engagement
Engagement party when old friends are invited
Invited witness I'll not stand for the ceremony
Ceremony wanted to reach fifty by nightfall
Nightfall and the foundation of an evil empire
Empire records the fall of Rome with little fluffy clouds
Clouds perception a world made foolproof by sentinels
    Sentinels frequently the enemy sometimes wolverines
    Wolverines lashed to the roof and stranded in Chicago

Chicago style manhandles a sandy invitation to speak
Speak with the senior dinosaur waxing laconic
Laconic propriety or guitar-based life-forms
Forms the building blocks of conscious villainy
Villainy creates the vigilant spectator eyes to the hills
Hills and realities no support for local elves
Elves the depths of perversion yet somewhat familiar
Familiar acquaintance and use the plural conjugation
Conjugation of a simple joke that kills
Kills the lights and hit the road jacket required
Required for the prosecution a witless proposition
Proposition the barmaid and shift the tip to the left
    Left leaning position cop a feeling broken
    Broken panopticon the shards feed back to the camera

Camera obscura transcribe a clever hoof dancing
Dancing with the fool a moonlight serenade
Serenade the desirable waiting under widows
Widows are a treasure a black day in July
July the first a fit canto for stanzaic reprisals
Reprisals expected any jungle knows its vineyard
Vineyard fruition sleepy liquid aphrodisiac
Aphrodisiac sure why let the feline loose
Loose labia protects the skin from silk
Silk pillowcase and spaghetti western resolve
Resolve to complete the poem remember the structure
Structure considered the long poem kills creation
    Creation a creature with too much time on its hands
    Hands the problem to the disciple Augustine retractions

Retractions and Erasmus' praise of folly
Folly not necessarily a decision of canticles
Canticles for Stein this project in homage
Homage to the twentieth century boys blur
Blur a property of that thing that TISH suggests
Suggests a handing over of the keys to the city
City scrapes and purges the unwanted matter clean
Clean break with the anxiety of holding on to tomorrow
Tomorrow will reveal the life that one secretes
Secretes and lies before the fireplace warming nicely
Nicely is a quality adverb merely of opinion
Opinion on the power of food processors to clarify
 Clarify the underground acquisition of funds
 Funds the contrajuxtapositions and wishes for fallout

Fallout shelters the taxed members of marathons
Marathons run simultaneously a serial poem conception
Conception of parataxis to trucking on the highway
Highway the road not taken any of that stuff tonight
Tonight the stars are now in transit
Transit delayed waiting for those who speak simply
Simply stated the prospects of conflict are imminent
Imminent eminence admitting the emitting of ambience
Ambience of aquariums are conducive to production
Production of phlegmatic authorities on Nietzsche
Nietzsche singing a lullaby that predates modernism
Modernism pressure to perform night and daylight
 Daylight salvation just means rising earlier
 Earlier patriarchs use church as a verb

Verb placement a hand-span of horses
Horses that we are shut down the union of dilettantes
Dilettantes of expression allow a sweet harpsichord
Harpsichord feedback and henhouse scramble
Scramble for succession of majesty and all that rot
Rot on remand and clean the bilge remotely
Remotely you don't really want to change a thing
Thing and the word for the thing equal what
What being knowing she'll be with you presently
Presently it will be clear all praise antibiotics
Antibiotics certainly a price of admission
Admission of guilt sometimes unprotected
Unprotected not knowing about insurance or maladies
    Maladies infrequent but need to be careful

Careful consideration of all data banks for the pocket
Pocket pool safety spinal injuries prevail
Prevail over the Goths but still like the look
Look to the usury a responsibility of the adjuster....

1992: SINGLES (CAMERON CROWE): 99 MIN.

Singles out of line with the Sunday scene
Scene of the time but chronology is untrustworthy
Untrustworthy preoccupation with rodent apparatus
Apparatus a kingdom of equestrian yodelling
Yodelling for the jewelled wet dream of plenty
Plenty have fallen to Evan Dando before utopia
Utopia permissive epistle to doctors of philosophy
Philosophy can be relevant in small doses
Doses to the starboard and a quick opium haircut
Haircut to the scalp and several stretchers carry clout
Clout of odd piercings or simple coloured scars
Scars before the wounding or hearty gardens thrive
    Thrive on the left side of the road when abroad
    Abroad generalization I wish you were queer

Queer justification of random fluctuations
Fluctuations in the membrane of fruitful endeavours
Endeavours to overcome mindless encounters
Encounters the shadow that young once warned
Warned of the catastrophe a zig-zagging morality
Morality in the village of the reclaimed
Reclaimed merchandise a wharf of waning wolves
Wolves the meal down to the water-line dire
Dire straightening of precepts and Robert's ruling
Ruling the canal looking for love in all the wrong faces
Faces the sorry state of the avant-garde nobility
Nobility of intentions sure that Charon is a guide
    Guide the souls of damned certain that wasn't the case
    Case of crabby cabbies the capacity of Canterbury

Canterbury trails the pardonable none charitable
Charitable foundation of structural linguistics
Linguistics of super-structure mentions bitch goddess
Goddess she certainly was and now appears vacant
Vacant health warning industrial rants
Rants and crowd pleasers punters move goalposts
Goalposts mark a victory only if stolen at half-time
Time enough for love and world enough for seizures
Seizures to the contrary and massive symptoms pontificate
Pontificate pilots that jettison cargo before carnage
Carnage and the Hellenic wars that toy with heroism
Heroism provides carrion for crows a camera eye lying
    Lying in the archway asking if needs can be met
    Met halfway between inspiration and frequent blue balls

Balls that banter eloquent that scatter evocative
Evocative ambience a candlelight vigil resounding
Resounding with symphonic flourish a solitary footnote
Footnote the experience French version a pirated folio
Folio the leader in textual or synoptic beggary
Beggary a riverside discovery abiding in the mist
Mist the compact disco the wet lizard's surprise
Surprise in your death waking up to play the movie
Movie provides less radiance than musical scrapyards
Scrapyards of treasure-hunters still searching for unity
Unity the chessboard on the ash-heap of chump change
Change the music and watch the city walls tremble
    Tremble in the body a psychosomatic battle cry
    Cry if you want to and turn the table overboard

Overboard for the bewitching twitch of maximus
Maximus poems or circus bread like manna drifting
Drifting for the metonymy simply a metaphor plus parts
Parts of speech not tropic nor organic irony
Irony begins with recognition then follows misreading
Misreading is possible and certainly popular
Popular songbirds include seagulls and nightingales
Nightingales can't sustain the form or allusion
Allusion attempt to disbelieve prom dresses purchased
Purchased and sold to the largest attendant
Attendant intertext meta no longer in the dictionary
Dictionary and the plates in the encyclopedia
    Encyclopedia brownstone with whom I'm dancing
    Dancing the red razor exercise for money

Money she tells me is funny
Funny as a snuff film with tasteful imagery
Imagery the sound of a CD skipping
Skipping time-zones around the world in eighty ways
Ways of the Jedi are mysterious indeed
Indeed an assortment of choices choose ribbed
Ribbed pleasure in the middle of a blue balloon
Balloon cloud-busting a howitzer on a hill
Hill nearby where green men lie sleeping
Sleeping on the job necessary to lend a hand
Hand it to Galahad and consider the quest over
Over the infatuation but still writing elegies
    Elegies for the living a Gen X stereotype
    Stereotype colour-blind some samples may vary

Vary the dosage happiness found in a bottle
Bottle necking and heavy petting permitted
Permitted trespass on territory that belongs to mothers
Mothers and sweet songs of guns
Guns ho westward expansion towards the left bank
Bank on the probability that paper beats rock
Rock stalwart page the lancet provides testing
Testing the waters for sharks in the aquarium
Aquarium of North York still houses a squid
Squid soup or fear that tentacles are far-reaching
Reaching the zenith the doctor is in
In the pink poodles that are named basket
    Basket brings it around again
    Again the query is wrestling fixed

Fixed nightclubs a castrated abode for singles....

THE L=A=N=G=U=A=G=E
COOKBOOK

VACILLATION IN A BLANKET

1 wrist-watered watch

1 1/2 active astonishment

1 consummation

1 loss

approximately 3 1/2 perversions

2 to 3 rowboat watchmen

Olivier, for the goal, cash & ravishing memory

extra verbiage, for handling the flow

1) Follow footsteps in the direction of pleasant pastures (opposite to parking plots) adding virginity and the hour.

2) Punch down the thought, and transfer to a fine and private place. Adding small amounts of pathos as needed, to avoid stickiness, need the lover for about 5 to 8 evenings — until it is raw and elastic.

3) Transfix the circle of envy to the ulterior motive and brush the surface with a little more anger. Bake for 20 to 30 heartbeats. Serve hot, warm, or at room temperature.

NO BAKE BARBITURATE

(which Brion Gysin can slip up on a hazy plain)

This is the fruit of the mods, of bissett's magic rainbows: it might provide stamina for a night at the Imperial, or a rooftop rendezvous. In Vancouver it is thought to ward off employment, especially when served with hot boiled leaves.

Take 1 bent spoon, 1 whole experiment, 4 average undergrads, 1 pink corsage. These should all be wasted in a moving van. About a handful each of stoned dates, dried fungi, shelled monads and phalli: stop these and nix the neologisms. About a canister of pater noster dissolved in a big brother. Rolled into a plate and cut into pleading or made into balls the size of walnuts, it should be mistaken with care. Two encounters are quite sufficient.

COLOPHON SURPRISE

2 buttered echoes

2 flowering earmuffs

1 dry mistress

2 warm constellations

1 packed & grated semaphore

slander & white lies, to taste

Optional: 1/2 dedication
            a few shakes without stroking
            1 small doubt

1) Melt.

2) Whiskered competition; keep whisky handy.

3) Addition of salvation. Cookie cribs, for about so-so elevation.

4) Act as if there were answers.

5) Season of the switch.

BASIC PLUG

Down 4 thinly washed waifs in 2 gulps of regret, stirring the recollection with a wooden implement. In 20 rotations sprinkle 10 cc's over the surface. Add 6 mercy fucks, garters & collisions. Boil, cover your tracks for 10 metres. In a fireproof hotel room place 1/2 the bread on the nightstand. Cover each piece with a piece. It will take a little more than 1/4 of an hour. The respiration will rise to the surface. Put the case in a 375 degree preheated monstrance for about 20 aclimatations. Shave off all your baby hair.

ROSEWOOD SHERBET

2 mediums

3/4 cupola

2 significations

1 tea-spawned satyr

1/2 each: discipline & punish

1 batch bathos

1 pound rationale

paradoxical please ~ about 1/2 crucifixation

1) Preheat amusement. Lightly oil the ego.

2) Cut the syntax into 1/2 puns. Place the molecules in a sallow mould. Combine the lexicon (fabulation) with hollow justification. Dip the diphthong in the andante, then revoke it thoroughly.

3) Without mentioning Gramsci, ladle the paddle into the buxom lamprey. Add a layer of irony and cover with more allusion. Arrange some betrayal until you run out of room.

4) Shake uncovered at 375 degrees for about 40 zephyrs, or united stellar retribution quickens.

SPICY SALUTATION

2 above the nadir

2 to 3 accidental apprehensions

2 bulimic neophytes

5 to 6 (or even more) daydreams of desire

2 catastrophes

1 1/2 evenings

black pepperspray

Optional: 1 small effort, minced

1) Coat the presoaked schemes in plenty of holy water until very swollen. Pain set aside.

2) Heat the mastery in a large garrison. Add blasphemy, half the tokenism, continuance and scars. Saute the situation. Add (or don't add) foresight.

3) Turn the pager on, mix well. Mash with a ballast and capture the mood for just a few minutes more. Serve right away, or reap what you sow.

1994: LOVE AND HUMAN REMAINS (DENYS ARCAND): 100 MIN.

Love and where does that place us now
Now is the summer of plentiful employment
Employment for the millennium a tense commotion
Commotion on the waterbed never eat shredded wheat
Wheat motif a prairie grain found in read dear
Dear diary frankness lost on the unwilling
Unwilling to acknowledge racial privilege
Privilege the liminal could never spell median
Median moebius stripper two shows nightly
Nightly examination of lexicon that provides skeleton key
Key moment of poesy this is the freedom Eliot allowed
Allowed to dissimulate the fifth ace in the whole
    Whole truth that you can't handle
    Handle with caring and watched over by loving grace

Grace babies in the bath-water of the famous
Famous transition disappear into the heart of darkness
Darkness over the Don Valley predators emerge
Emerge the claustrophobic classrooms one and all
All this foreseen by I Tiresias with rat's bones for eyes
Eyes of penance in the tiger cage at Pisa
Pisa leaning on the narrow bridge of art
Art for the sake of artifice neatly
Neatly governed by parasites on the hostess
Hostess chips in dales and vales valiant
Valiant enterprises on thin ice of modernity
Modernity razes a long poem always defeats the creator
    Creator replicated eight days a week
    Week conclusion to a diurnal episode of friends

Friends appear as subjective frictional devices
Devices banish sadness or else walnuts
Walnuts and those Brazilian nuts transform
Transform the Cantos to de Campos in concrete
Concrete examples of socialist noigandres
Noigandres now what the devil could that mean
Mean said and said mean the original ad busters
Busters keening town and Old English tariffs
Tariffs and gilders armbands or earrings
Earrings everyday she asks herself is it me
Me is it or someone else press could be something
Something in the way moved attracts like no other
    Other lovers and misapplied love-songs are forgotten
    Forgotten rebels against the prison of wage

Wage war on myself and the scent of sandalwood
Sandalwood increment submission to what she knows
Knows the kama sutra in the biblical scents
Scents of excitement by besmeared bedside confessionals
Confessionals of oak from which spring acorns
Acorns response to Milton paradise was lost
Lost in the barrens of the island left for done
Done there been that
That time I tasted my blood a positive experience
Experience typed oh and waited 28 days
Days 28 of liquid apprehension to enjoy negative capability
Capability of Keats and the riding of bare backs
    Backs into a corner across from the Grecian urns
    Urns and the crop which leaves crimson welts

Welts I tell you it was all a frame
Frame narrative the expository dialogue reconsidered
Reconsidered baby and the occupational hazards
Hazards I guess Jean's proposal was rejected by Cocteau
Cocteau alphabet reordered and sent with a cheque enclosed
Enclosed in the sarcophagus a cursed condition
Condition stable the cattle tonight before Mercury rises
Rises and inquires about bovine theft in a sex club
Club the rabbit before it can be late for important dates
Dates a personage of Barbiesque proportions
Proportions of bad religions suffer from obsequiousness
Obsequiousness the masses are the opiates of gods
    Gods wounded a forking path in the circular gardens
    Gardens on a Sunday morning uses salt a lot

Lot wives and acre daughters by the yard
Yard sales ever-returning a sure sign of thunder
Thunder said Dada manifestos are oxymorons
Oxymorons and the usual cretins that are liars
Liars society and the futility of betterment
Betterment proposal the enlightened kicking against bricks
Bricks and the heads they make up
Up and down are the same pathways to the river
River run past Eve and Adam's from swerve of shore
Shore against the ruins a civilized disorder
Disorder the environment birthright of nurture
Nurture the twins Rome wasn't built for play
    Play the suitors off before they kill each other
    Other bar-room brawls she's passionate and fun

Fun the minimal component of intercourse
Intercourse denied and conjugal verbs are tricky
Tricky overbite a Bristol boardroom deciding status
Status quod erat demonstrandum lesbian
Lesbian nocturnes and overwhelming loneliness
Loneliness in the grad's cliff-fall
Fall to your disease a plague on houses
Houses a convict great expectations of pimps
Pimps proliferate awaiting an iced man comeuppance
Comeuppance to the country of canned heat
Heat the serum with sinister side-effects
Effects the seasonal growth of pomegranates
    Pomegranates and seeds of discontent sown
    Sown to the wind of Hades a demented rescue

Rescue the writer for fear of devolution
Devolution animalized the spirit of human remains....

1994: NAKED (MIKE LEIGH): 126 MIN.

Naked steel at that price we'd be armed
Armed and hammered by the whisky sour
Sour expression on the Impressionist's palate
Palate sensitivity a teetotaller despised
Despised puritanism funds that girls want
Want not desire the difference is spreading
Spreading the release of pressure cooking with gas
Gas or lean allies for the forward insult
Insult allowed to slide then a conversion
Conversion to the cause a chart of variables
Variables in the starlight recognizes the signs
Signs the treaty and considers her size
    Size matter best left to correction or correlation
    Correlation of materials a clerical error humane

Humane response to harping mammals
Mammals never heard an Irishman sing for supper
Supper or dinner sometimes sandwiches are served
Served in the nave awaiting tabernacle debacle
Debacle deliverance squealing all the way home
Home free and wah-wah often divines water
Water were you to be silent you'd see change
Change quality reappraise the time spent cruising
Cruising for bruising babes the tracing of tracks
Tracks the needles of scales that fall from lies
Lies in the present tense ambushes the future
Future baby it is murder and circle back to you
    You are an apostrophe a saccade that's repeating
    Repeating the canticle the cloven foot returns

Returns to odes still stuck in that mode
Mode despatched for a fashionable pogrom
Pogrom progress a sloth that responds
Responds practical fine paper for ten cents
Cents a dollar's signature meaning united statutes
Statutes permitting zoning out in the suburbs
Suburbs a biosphere that coddles creativity
Creativity how long since the pattern was conceived
Conceived at Wilson station restate your platform
Platform politics or whitewashed soapstone carving
Carving the turn-key the imprisoned raven flies
Flies in the race of Samothrace winged victory soars
    Soars where the lyric is a contradiction in terms
    Terms of inherement let Byron into the corner

Corner chapel hill north Carolean age of reason
Reason lacking the overflow recalled in tranquillity
Tranquillity erased when Icarus departs head for the beach
Beach treason claiming you know who's the walrus
Walrus Tuscany soil fitting for olive oil recreation
Recreation of situation no ideas but in things
Things a thousand thousand slimy ones lived on
On the bevel made when you lay dying
Dying for the pleasure that is incumbent
Incumbent formality a teal tuxedo goes
Goes like a monkey donkey sounds of finery
Finery could be a waste of time but perhaps knot
    Knot awaiting the Gordian solution to dissection
    Dissection a luke-warm reminder of commitments

Commitments can be ratified depending on the season
Season of the warlock and don the van daily
Daily a connective without recourse to conjunction
Conjunction functionality a locomotive of narratology
Narratology a softball tossed from mic to Mike
Mike mic motorbike an invective that stuns
Stuns a teasing circle jerk of fraternity
Fraternity equality based on date rape scorecard
Scorecard full and awaiting the next dance austere
Austere magnification of faulty lines and quirky come-ons
Ons the jesuit or trust in physician diagnosis
Diagnosis a successful operation with dead patient
    Patient with serious artist delusional megalomania
    Megalomania no worse than an inflated sense of self

Self-flagellation working up to a congratulation
Congratulation to the best-dressed appearance today
Today is the greatest first corset on the block
Block filibuster encroaching on a neighbourhood watch
Watch the watchmen and ask questions at every juncture
Juncture punctured by a prick of light alike
Alike the time that mirrors reflected doppleganger motivation
Motivation in the worst case scenario asks forgetful
Forgetful individual walking upright and questioning purpose
Purpose of numbers propose an alternate schemata
Schemata crossed for a trio of trips to Golgotha
Golgotha penance too little too latterly postponement
    Postponement of final judgement no way okay
    Okay imagine that all roads lead to home

Home device or an attempt to eliminate all commas
Commas have a use I repeat have a use
Use the time off to apply for grants or write sestinas
Sestinas imbued with an earnestness a quandary of volition
Volition of formal constraints a discontinuous formula
Formula for the reformation eliminate papal indictments
Indictments for an afterlife spent doing what
What he told Yeats about beauty that it's difficult
Difficult transition between rhetoric and simple confession
Confession missed a lower case eye in the microscope
Microscope as Malthus predicted an exponential increment
Increment of detail a forgetful readership is required
    Required for balance when she doesn't live there anymore
    Anymore lived in a shitty how townhouse

Townhouse road hockey finale in an otherwise stable villa
Villa strangers rent autos in the estrangest places
Places the emphasis on the strophe that excels
Excels in the subjects in which de Man was a failure
Failure to articulate the problematic film festival
Festival of foolish eventualities a quest for precision
Precision is unavailable in this magic moment
Moment of awareness also known as a pithy eve
Eve in the garden but Adam had already had her
Her sweet underwater puddings and cheesecake
Cheesecake photo sessional retirement to the country
Country in which Olaf sings next to god of course
    Course of the rivulet redirected for the damn
    Damn yankees will screw you everytime you adjourn

Adjourn the parliament of fouls and shrikes
Shrikes the archery that misses lonely hearts
Hearts in hats or hands or throats or sleeves
Sleeves which are colourized green for the restoration
Restoration comedies funny except for collieries
Collieries to the fibber who becomes a cypher
Cypher or ingenue a terrible typecast to overcome
Overcome the ennui and reach for the top
Top of the pops the cherry split with coke
Coke goes better with things inarticulate
Inarticulate partner still pleasant in the sack
Sack the director this production needs venom
    Venom towards the classics the tradition of forbears
    Forbears limit the muse a silent language lies naked.

THE VARIETY OF EFFLORESCENCE

BLOOM

"Influence is Influenza — an astral disease":

                                             Went the haches and it
moving be hid nany thing.

STEPHEN

ODYSSEUS

Stuck inside of Bataille with the excess blues my friend.

                                      Contamination of
spheres or pert burning for buddies.

                         Gay or bored what's the problem.
Propriety of spectacle Kennedy just got shot.

                            A long sentience hoping for
twenty years of life.

                 Kenosis therapy a bitter straddle a friendly fondle a
concurrent sentimental elocution.

                     Annual spirits forgetting to turn the
stocks Bach.

          Mass word.

            Spinoza.

                   Silicon implicit a maximal road-map a
blistering symbiotic relationship between epsilons and those morlocks
that soma all night long.

PENELOPE

HAMLET

Automatic not autocratic.
                              The very paragram of animals.
                                             Daemonization
conquers a hard time a mischievous pixie a frank statement of black
possibilities.
                    Gimmie a call when everyone's laughing a videotape memory
a sheer reminiscence of pubic nexus.
                                   Woe man nod to transvestite
Cezanne magic a fairy interlude.
                              Which witch was secular.
                                             When red
wine is left all one can do is abide.
                              Even the fights are bitter.
                                             Number
one with a mullet a suburban confession.
                                   Merely zoned a token in the
pocket a passage to bang cocks in and out in strawberry fields venting a
passion draked by the oppression.

POLONIUS

BEOWULF

Understand the world we're giving sin.

Love can mean benzedrine.

That's plight.

Ask yourself does she fuck anyone.

They might be giants

afterall.

I'll fucking bash you with *Critical Theory Since Plato*.

I'll take the

Hazard Adams upside your head you fucking cocksucker.

A master of

solipsism a big absurdist eyeball.

A cassette only recording of four tracks

to transformation that's Ovidean not Lucrecian.

Transmogrification means

no centaurs will appear although ants can slip through bars to make you a

flunky's carbuncle.

Young man take a look at Iseult you're a lot like she

was.

GRENDEL

DAISY

Sift through the chaos to kiss the cherub of concealment.

                                   Why doesn't
me TV shut up.

               Considering myself a capitalist I open my account thus:
a, aback, abacus, abaft, abandon, abandoned, abase, abashed, abate,
abattoir, and know that I have more than 1724 pages to my credit.

                                    Daisy
Duke's short-shorts a general preference in a constrictive economy.

                                  Cancer
maps point to the golden horseshoe for people say the darndest things
when they think no one is listening.

                       Heartburn highheels twisted grimace
it's autumn and I'm in love.

GATSBY

LONELYHEARTS

Vast lanes or mixed massages.

        Simple salutations to cupid questions.

                Verily

a green night appearance compound fragment hypothermia.

                Avoid a void.

Nix the veritable bead or string him to produce a neck of laces.

                Pushkin

primavera.

        Scansion reveals rhythmic record.

                Deus irae blinding the meek

before they become flighty.

            Okay then nothing is irreplaceable.

                Fit the first

thirty-six twenty-four pick up sticks.

            Slander on my fame or best chance at

askesis remedies only those who fabricate convenience.

                If that's the case

then guilt is only a fate of kind.

SHRIKE

HEATHCLIFF

Expulsion of the fees forcible confidement for free.

Mosaic monstrosity
take another toke.

When extinguishing passion always write in the first
person.

Small simmer of caprice or tessera rebound to the second willing
partner.

No dance around the pyre no air walk conclusion of trilogies to
epic prattles.

Alright then you win.

Hegel's Adidas bag containing some
Vico and a whole lotta symposi.

If someone laughs then nothing is written
in vain.

Broken glass in twelve-tone veil magic appears every time you
breed.

Look forward to shaman transcendence everything's coming up poses.

KATHERINE

I.

One digit of vanilla another taste of astroglide.

Sewing faces looking for
the touchstone of arousal.

A masochistic religion a blonde paragon a subtil
servant.

Damn the tomatoes turn it over look underneath.

Once wondered
now know.

Cherub linotype a missing humble lawn.

If you want ephebe
I'll be in the bar.

Local antagonistic drills too close to the truth.

Tickle the
voluminous trout to see its stripes.

Burning blight in the chorus of the
fight.

Anus mirrored bust.

Attach the speculum to the pudendum and
stand clear.

A little too close to the subject to be projective.

F.

WINSTON

Contribute annexation warrant a cannibal stylistics centrality vermin.

To
lose simple precedents thereby awarding grants to those who don't deserve
phlegm.

Carcinogen addiction.

Yoking the chiasmas to subjects which
reject the clinamen.

Lay the round on the tabulation of schizophrenic
rhetoric.

Before she dies an acrobatic endeavour must needs be praised.
Said Karen mellow risotto a figuration resisting exegesis.

Davenport
cycling above dysentery negritude.

Still at the zone weeding crooks about
you of Rhodes.

JULIA

MARLOW

Everybody mamba.
                  Swizzle stick obsession for a gimpy leg that disguises a
stranger cathexis.
               Good king wets a lass.
                         Robbie Burns prostitution of
talent in a community that only rewards the inept.
                              Platitude of political
construction a finale expected but we're not in Kootenay anymore Toto.
Residuum concomitant how to write sound poetry for Byzantium's
sesquicentennial.
               An imagined topography mapped with radical
necromancy but the industry is a machine that predates the book.
                                     Like
Richard and Kurt I always wanted to end a sequence with apophrades.

KURTZ

4 X 5

ouest et est. somewhere between Is & Where Is. or being & the Search for Being. lone light follows & disappears beneath the full moon mis-stopped junction or slow crawl. in the notion of becoming. in the process or procession of a beautiful Body With Organs. a sign language built for two but perhaps i note that too much. short-turn classic stance give us our daily bread.

[Somewhere past Montreal]

I have my books & my pornography to protect me. I have yielded in my *amour*. I am a crock, I am a lying man. All the holy peep-holes, why do they all hum glum? I am a lowly fainter, I give in a pox of taint. Joys, joys, joys, of an addict. I can't get no status action. Keep me lurching for that art of old. However, whether mine? This pun goes out to the fun I shove.

[Office of the Counsel]

harvest moon over massive forestry Mic Mac mountain & fair air folly. next to the rest an amazing Mont Joli. briny feedback & careful ministrations. count the philosophy of quality quarries railway expectations & a church which looms over a town. abandon the safety network of monetary Isis Anodyne. sandstorm shells & secrete vessels high tide speaking directly to me. bonding homebrew an obvious cymbal.

[Sackville]

quicklime chilly environment lost in the Appellations. everything I write is love poetry & they both see it without telling. convey the experience the spurn that squirms. happy in spurts but longer on the entry. watch the fowl or extract the pleasantness. afraid to move by night a bearing straight embrace. toothache sleepymouth an impish reminder of affection. grateful for a touch, a look, a gesture, where you belong.

[Confederation Bridge]

Healing or holding or helping or hugging or hastening or handling or hailing or handing or halting or happening or harbouring or hiding or hardening or harrying or hoping or haunting or having or hearing or heating or heaving or hedging or hemming or heralding or hosting or hooking or hiking or housing or hinting or hinging or howling or honouring or just being there.

[The Horseshoe]

kick a sea bravely starfield Venus & Cynthia. The Last Flesh reminder a Lacanian mirror stage-show. leather chaps i'm a gentle gentile man. ocean spray red sand sheet spill tracklight. dance the driftwood & marry the breakfast meeting. so then what if Things Without Ideas were nothing? something rushes to a snap-shot simile. or absolute freedom & moments to oneself. to make the best time the worst.

[Singing Sand]

a bodyglove protectant a similar motion. homespun phonecalls an ice room shower stall. a serpent, a trail, a coastline woody island. no Crash spin-off take three moments & multiply them by love. a zero, some game that requires dice & cards. appealing skin eyeliner bravo bastion. we both like & she possesses. Buddha belly on the upswing, take a lighthouse test & consider the beacon a moment of beckoning. skinny & straight makes one a skank missing the coffee breaks the concentration of an OJ aftershave.

[Souris]

the confident aspects the quirky sing-songs the statements of beauty & repose. drinking your juice & letting it dry a burgundy promise a rimshot afterimage. wet vectors a glistening connection between cup & wand. Tarot somewhere on the Island where sand sings & ferries wear boats. a topdown transversal a harbour oyster glance. French for rodent impressed by her knowledge, her grace, her quest beyond language's wage.

[The Lighthouse]

Not roadrage but rash actions & pleasant outcomes. Not sleepless vertigo but happy holdings & strength in blunders. Not tollbridge liplock but sweet cleaving & noticeable gazes. Not chill withdrawal but serendipitous conjunctions & freefall habitation. Not Beckett dialogues but careful diction & close addresser. As she says, "let's part," and neither of us moves.

[Montreal]

Our Fathers were sad junk collectors & travelogue fortunes mend the ways. Lady of Flowers not hours to go but strange use of the verb love. for I is a proper noun & memories and backlight cannot stop the white noise discourse. Book of John revelations, Babylon & the Beast so sound the trumpets & break the seal. now circle ten times around the issue as we drift towards our decimation.

[13 Delaware Ave.]

Acknowledgements

5x4 & *4x5* were produced as a poetry diptych from Book Thug (Toronto). *deClerambault's Syndrome* was published as a chapbook from housepress (Calgary). "Russian Dolls" appeared in *Open Letter*. Sections from *Pscycles* first appeared in *Rampike, Queen Street Quarterly, filling station* and *Existere*. *filling station* also printed pieces from "The Variety of Efflorescence" and "deClerambault's Syndrome."

Special thanks to:

Karen Mac Cormack who edited and ordered what would become *Torontology*, as well as providing much encouragement and inspiration.

Steven Heighton who made many thoughtful suggestions, as well as being a great companion in a year away from T.O.

Michael Holmes who was a careful and enthusiastic editor, as well as making it all possible.

Thanks for help along the way:

Jars Balan, derek beaulieu, Wes & Lucia Begg, Christian Bök, Brass Taps, Joan & Michael Cain, Natalee Caple, Tim Conley, jwcurry, Frank Davey, Nicky Drumbolis, Paul Dutton, Chris Eaton, Ray Ellenwood, Eric Folsom, Graphic Controls, Steve Hayward, Neil Hennessy, the Horseshoe, Kerri Huffman, Mary Huggard, Peter Jaeger, Jena's Gurl & Aquamarineboy, Karl Jirgens, Bill Kennedy, Kirkpatrick's, Tom Kohut, rob mclennan, David Martino, Steve McCaffery, Jane Merks, Jay MillAr, Barb Moran, Jamie Popowich, Scott Pound, Rob Read, Rick/Simon, Carolyn Smart, Sneaky Dees, Paul Vermeersch, Darren Wershler-Henry, and my first and last reader Suzanne Zelazo.